THE DOMINIE WORLD OF ANIMALS

RHINOS

Graham Meadows & Claire Vial

Contents

DOMINIE PRESS
Pearson Learning Group

About Rhinos

Rhino is another word for *rhinoceros*. Rhinos have been around since **prehistoric** times, more than forty million years ago. Some of their ancestors were larger than elephants; others were as small as wolves. They lived in Europe, North America, Africa, and Asia.

Today there are only five **species** of rhinos left. Indian, Sumatran, and Javan rhinos live in Asia. White rhinos and black rhinos live in Africa. All of these species are in danger of becoming **extinct**.

This book is about the white rhino.

Swahili is a language that is spoken in many parts of East Africa. The Swahili word for *rhinoceros* is *faru*.

Their Shape and Size

The white rhino is the second-largest land mammal in the world. The elephant is the largest.

In many ways, the white rhino still looks like a prehistoric animal. Its huge, barrel-shaped body is covered by thick, gray skin that looks like armor.

The hump on the white rhino's neck contains the strong muscles that hold up its large head. It has small eyes, big ears, large nostrils, and a wide, square mouth.

The word *white* does not describe the rhino's color. It comes from the Dutch word *weit*, which means *wide*. It describes the rhino's very wide **muzzle**.

Their Shape and Size

An adult male rhino can be up to six feet high at the shoulders. Its body can be up to fifteen feet long and weigh up to 5,000 pounds. Females are smaller and can weigh up to 3,500 pounds. This huge weight is supported by four short, strong legs.

A rhino's tail can be up to three feet long.

A male rhino is called a bull. A female is called a cow. A baby rhino is called a calf.

Their Horns

The white rhino has two horns on top of its nose. The horn in front is longer than the one behind it. The front horn is usually about two feet long, but it can grow up to five feet in length. It has a wide base and curves upward and backward, ending in a point.

The back horn is shaped like a triangle and is usually less than one foot long.

Just like our fingernails and hair, a rhino's horns grow throughout its life.

The word *rhinoceros* comes from two Greek words— *rhinos*, which means *nose*, and *keros*, or *horn*.

Their Feet

Rhinos have three toes on each foot. Each toe has a toenail. The middle toes are the largest. They support most of the rhino's weight.

There is a thick, rubbery pad about twelve inches wide on the bottom of each foot. This pad acts as a cushion and spreads out the animal's weight when it is walking or running.

Rhinos walk at about three miles an hour. They trot at about eighteen miles an hour. Over a short distance, a rhino can run as fast as thirty miles an hour.

Their Eyes, Ears, and Noses

Rhinos can't see very well, and their eyes are very small. Because their eyes are on the sides of the head, they can't focus on anything straight ahead of them. In order to see more clearly, a rhino will turn its head sideways and use one eye.

Although they have poor eyesight, rhinos have very good hearing and an excellent sense of smell to alert them to danger. First, they move their large ears to find out where a sound is coming from. Then they use their sense of smell to find out what made the sound and whether or not it means they are in danger.

A rhino can smell a **predator** up to half a mile away.

Their Skin

Rhinos often roll in mud to stay cool. When the mud dries on their skin, it helps to protect them from sunburn and biting insects. The mud also makes it more difficult for **parasites** to live on their skin. If they can't find any mud, rhinos will roll in dust.

Birds called oxpeckers, or tick birds, often perch on rhinos and pick the ticks off their skin. Other birds, called egrets, are often found near rhinos, eating the insects that stir when the huge mammals move around.

Their Diet

The white rhino is a **herbivore**, which means it eats plants. The main part of the rhino's **diet** is grass. Because it has no front teeth, it uses the muscular lips on its wide mouth to clip off blades of grass. Then it chews the grass with its large back teeth, or **molars**.

Rhinos spend about half the day grazing, usually during the early morning, in the evening, or at night, when it is cool.

Rhinos can eat more than 100 pounds of vegetation every day.

Their Diet

Rhinos drink up to twenty-five **gallons** of water a day, so they like to stay close to a water hole or some other source of water. They often drink in the morning or in the evening, when it is cool. A rhino will walk as far as fifteen miles to find water. It can **survive** for as long as three days without drinking if it has to.

When it is very dry, rhinos can use their front feet to dig holes and reach water that is under the ground.

Their Families

Female rhinos **mate** when they are about six years old and give birth about sixteen months later. Usually only one calf is born at a time. Twins are rare. Before she gives birth, a female leaves the **herd** and moves into thick bushes for protection.

Female rhinos and their calves often form small herds of six to eight animals. Male rhinos generally live alone. They join a herd only to mate. Males often fight with other males to defend their **territory**.

A female rhino gives birth to a calf every two to three years.

Their Young

When it is born, a white rhino calf weighs about 110 pounds. Within an hour, the calf can stand up and **suckle**, or drink its mother's milk. The calf will start to **graze** when it is about eight weeks old, but it will not be **weaned** until it is about one year old.

Rhino calves gain up to six pounds a day. They weigh as much as 1,000 pounds by the time they are just one year old.

A rhino calf usually stays with its mother until it is two to three years old. Then it carries on the amazing story of these massive creatures—a story that started millions of years ago.

Glossary

diet:	The food that an animal or person usually eats
extinct:	No longer alive; species of animals or plants that have disappeared
gallons:	One gallon is equal to four quarts
graze:	To eat, or feed on plants
herbivore:	An animal that eats plants
herd:	Groups of animals that have a common bond and live together like a family
mate:	To join with another animal in order to produce offspring
molars:	Teeth with rounded or flattened surfaces used for grinding
muzzle:	An animal's mouth and nose
parasites:	Animals that live on other animals and use them to survive
predator:	An animal that hunts and kills other animals
prehistoric:	Before recorded time; a very, very long time ago
species:	Types of animals that have something in common
suckle:	To drink a mother's milk
survive:	To stay alive
Swahili:	A language that is spoken in many parts of East Africa
territory:	An area that is occupied and defended by an animal or group of animals
weaned:	No longer drinking a mother's milk; able to find and eat other food

Index